A Special

TO: _____

FROM: _____

DATE: _____

Scott Simpson • Larry Mize
Loren Roberts

F*The*OCUS

Name

of the

Game with Sigmund Brouwer

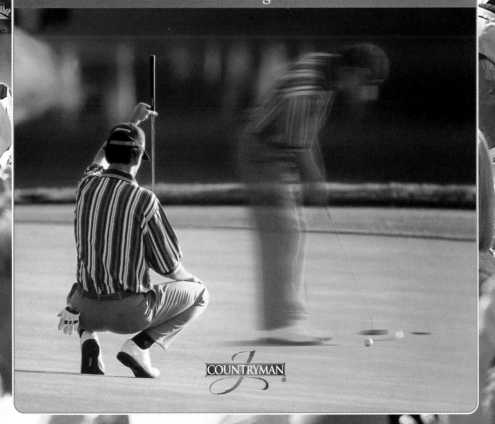

COUNTRYMAN

Designed by Koechel Peterson, Inc., Minneapolis, Minnesota

Photography by Tom Henry, Koechel Peterson, Inc., Minneapolis, MN

Printed and bound in Belgium

ISBN: 08499-5505-X

FOCUS *Table of Contents*

Foreword

Introduction

Larry Mize: *The Woods*

The Swing

Shotmaking

Golf Strategy

Life Strategy

Faith

Flashbacks

Scott Simpson: *The Irons*

The Swing

Shotmaking

Golf Strategy

Life Strategy

Faith

Flashbacks

Loren Roberts: *The Short Game*

The Swing

Shotmaking

Golf Strategy

Life Strategy

Faith

Flashbacks

Player Profiles

FOCUS *Foreword*

From the Publisher...

Focus — *The Name of the Game* is a book J. Countryman has been looking forward to publishing for some time. In it, Larry Mize, Loren Roberts, and Scott Simpson share their secrets of success in golf and in life. These three wonderful professionals, who have been on the PGA Tour for a total of sixty-two years, demonstrate how "Focus" is necessary to improving your golf game as well as keeping your life in balance. These very talented golfers have won, between them, sixteen tournaments, including two majors (the Masters and the U.S. Open). Their total financial rewards have been, to date, $17,874,670.

But greater than this is their moment-by-moment walk with the Lord and their dependence on Him for strength and reassurance. These men share with us that the only way for them to have a complete sense of peace and happiness is through their relationship with a loving and forgiving God.

Our prayer is that this book will help you, not only with your golf game, but we pray that it will also help deepen your faith as you "Focus" on our awesome God, who loves each of us with an everlasting love.

Jack Countryman

FOCUS *Introduction*

Golf, like life, is about discipline and struggle through the highs and lows of triumph and defeat. It is about *focus*. Focus on short-term lessons. Focus on long-term goals. *Focus on the prize that really matters.*

For successful professional golfers like Larry Mize, Scott Simpson, and Loren Roberts, their focus has resulted in a combined total of 16 PGA victories, including Mize's dramatic Masters win at Augusta and Simpson's hard-fought U.S. Open Championship.

This book is where they discuss their own focus keys — on the course and off.

You will learn from Larry Mize how to hit better and longer drives; from Scott Simpson how to hit irons like a pro; from Loren Roberts how to cut strokes around the green. Learn from them all savvy course management that will help you take strokes off your score.

As they reflect on their focus keys to faith and life, it will seem like you've pulled up a chair and joined them at the clubhouse at the end of a round. Read about the shots that gave them victories and about shots that cost them tournaments. Read about what matters most to them — because victory and defeat have taught each of them many lessons. What they've learned most is that fame and money are not enough. "And whatever you do, do it heartily, as to the Lord and not to men" (Colossians 3:23).

Sigmund Brouwer

F(The)OCUS
Woods
Larry Mize

Few athletes have the *grace under pressure* to define themselves or their careers in a single moment that becomes etched into the history of their sport. For Larry Mize, a 140-foot chip-in to end a sudden death play-off at the 1987 Masters became that moment. Seen thousands upon thousands of times in television replays since, the perfection of his sand wedge on the 11th hole at Augusta overshadows what most people forget — Mize's gritty come-from-behind performance to get into the play-off against legends Greg Norman and Seve Ballesteros, including a clutch birdie on the final hole of regulation play.

Indeed, his first PGA tour victory in 1983 came with a 25-foot putt on the 18th hole. A Ryder Cup player, all of his other tour victories resulted from accuracy off the tee and shots under pressure that allowed him to overtake tournament leaders in the final stretches of competition.

Bright as his golf shines, however, Larry Mize has discovered that *meaning in his life comes from another source of light.* Join him for a walk through golf, and discover how his focus can help you on and off the course . . .

> *"Let your light so shine before men, that they may see your good works and glorify your Father in heaven."*
>
> MATTHEW 5:16

The Swing

Accuracy with the Driver

One of my *focus keys* to keeping a drive on the fairway is *good tempo*. I try to play within myself. The pros only swing to about 80 percent of their full power on most tee shots. Only if I can get there in two on a par 5, or if the fairway is wide, will I reach back to swing big.

In other words, don't get up to the tee box and see how far you can hit it. Make sure your swing is under control. Keep this in mind, and you'll have the key to hitting a good drive or any good shot — the key is making solid contact.

How do you know if you've swung too hard? By whether you keep your balance after your swing. If you start falling all over the place, you are out of good tempo.

In fact, when I finish my swing, I want to be able to hold my finish position for about a count of five, which is more difficult than you might think. Doing this will tell you a lot about your swing and help you with your balance.

The Takeaway

Before hitting a drive, I take a last waggle of the club head over the ball to release tension and get a little rhythm in the shot. After that last waggle I don't let much time pass before I swing. Because if I stop that waggle I'll become stagnant. From there, I press my hands forward to initiate the whole swing. Other people, like Gary Player, kick the right knee in. You want to find a small trigger movement with the body or hands to get the swing started.

Load Your Swing to the Top

You need to make a good weight transfer. At the top of your backswing, make sure you have turned into your right side, and that you have the majority of your weight on your right foot — that is, get your left shoulder over your right knee. By putting it there, you have completed your shoulder turn.

You want to *turn* around your right leg — you don't want any sliding. Especially with the driver or *any of the long clubs*, you really need to make sure to get behind the ball.

Don't worry that your head must remain still. If you look at the majority of the top players, *their heads move* two to three inches as they complete the backswing.

Say It Again. . .
The Head *Moves*
Behind the Ball?

Unless you set up like Jack Nicklaus, with your head cocked and way back to the right, your head is going to have to move to the right in the backswing. Then you must keep your head behind the ball on the way down; don't let it move forward of its position at address.

Initiate the Downswing

With the first move to the ball, make a slight lateral or sideways move to get the weight back onto the left side. Without this, you run the risk of "spinning out" — clearing your hips before you get to your left side, with the result that all the weight is on your back foot and you've made a reverse pivot. After moving your weight to the left side, you can now rotate your hips and generate a lot of speed. Larry Nelson once put it this way: "It's like standing on your right foot, until you shift your weight to your left foot. Everybody can do it."

The Swing

The Downswing

The downswing starts from the ground up. Think of getting your weight to the ball of the left foot and from there your hips begin to rotate. As your hips begin to rotate, pull your hands into the correct position to come from the inside and swing the club down the line. If you *focus* on getting the weight to the ball of the left foot, from there you can rotate as fast as you want and just let it go.

The Swing

Clear the Hips

Clearing *the hips* simply means rotating the hips through the shot. When you get through swinging, your belt buckle should be pointed at the target, or even left of the target.

Avoid...Using the Arms

If you start that downswing with your arms, your club head will move at the ball from the outside-in. The club face will come across the ball, and you will either hit a big pull or a big slice.

Focus Key:

As you rotate the hips, keep a connection between your upper arms and your chest. Your right arm must stay in front of your right hip. If your right arm gets trapped behind your right hip, you will be stuck from the inside and will lose power and accuracy. Then when your hands catch up, you can snap hook, or you can block the ball dead right.

Let your timing and the tempo work together to keep everything moving. The lower body starts, and immediately after, the upper body follows and whips through.

The Swing

The Follow-Through

The best follow-through is one where your hands end up immediately over your left shoulder. A lot of players want a high finish over the left ear, but if you look at the swings of the great players like Hogan or Nelson, their hands finish above the left shoulder. This finish ensures that your hands stay close to your body until after impact, helping you keep that important connection between chest and arms through the swing.

The Swing

Ball Placement

Everybody's swing is different, so you need to find the bottom of your arc, or with the driver, slightly ahead of the bottom. Generally speaking, this puts it somewhere between your left heel and your left toe.

For a big drive, move the ball slightly forward in your stance. It will help you get more aggressive and get more length.

The Difference Between
Driver & Fairway Woods

Since the ball is on a tee, play the driver slightly farther forward in your stance than a fairway wood. Other than that, there is little difference in the swing between drivers, fairway woods, and long irons.

Woods from a Fairway Bunker

Don't hit your fairway woods out of bunkers unless you really have to. I think you can take a 4- or 5-iron and probably do just as well.

If you are going to hit a fairway wood, dig your feet into the bunker to give yourself a nice firm stance, and make sure that you choke up on the club because with your feet into the ground, you are closer to the ball.

As you swing, concentrate on keeping your body steady. The sand may be sloppy around your feet, and your lower body will have a tendency to move. To counteract this, use less shoulder turn and a little shorter backswing.

A cut shot — outside-in swing — is going to come out of a bunker better because you will have less chance of taking too much sand. A fat or heavy shot out of the bunker is disastrous, but if you hit the ball thin — catching more ball than sand — you might still get away with it, unless the bunker has a big lip directly in front of you. If you move the ball slightly back in the stance, it will then help your swing catch the ball first.

Hit a Draw or Fade

The easiest way to draw or fade the ball is to adjust the angle of the club face. Aim the club face where you want the ball to land. Then line your body parallel to the target line where you want your ball to begin. With a draw, for example, this might be 30 feet right of the hole. When you put your hands on the club and look down, the club face will be hooded because your body is lined up right. Make a regular swing, and the hooded club face puts right-to-left spin, producing a draw.

It is, of course, the reverse to fade or slice. When you aim the club face with where you want the ball to land, line up your body along a target line parallel left.

With these small changes in body and club face alignment, a good swing will always give you good results.

Avoid...Double Cross

There is nothing worse than the dreaded "double cross" — trying to hit a fade and instead hitting a draw. You've aimed left expecting the ball to go right, and it goes even farther left, getting you in deeper trouble.

The key to avoiding this is practice. Get on the driving range, hit two draws, hit two fades, and keep alternating.

The Swing Difference
Between Driver & Irons

With the shorter irons, you need to place the ball farther back in the stance, closer to the middle. I don't play anything behind the middle of my stance unless I am trying a *knock-down shot*. Other than that I don't make any changes with my swing. You don't want to practice or do two swings; it is just too difficult.

Remember, the club itself makes the difference. With shorter clubs, the swing will be more upright because the ball is closer to you.

The key with short irons is to be accurate and to control your distance. Because these are the "scoring" clubs, you should practice a lot with them. If you can hit the short irons well, swings with all the other clubs are just an extension of that, so spend a lot of your practice time on wedges and 9-, 8-, and 7-irons. After all, if you get a 7-iron or less in your hand, you want to hit the ball close to the pin.

Fairway Woods out of the Rough

Unless you have a really good lie, you shouldn't use a wood to hit out of the rough. If the rough is really high, you don't even want to try anything more than a 7-iron, because the risk-reward is not worth it. In other words, you need to simply take your lumps.

If you feel the rough is not that bad and you are determined to hit a wood, at least keep the 3-wood in your bag; hit with your 4-, 5-, 6-, or 7-wood instead.

The *main focus key* is to play a "cut" shot. If swinging inside-out — a draw — you come in from a lower angle, and the grass will grab your club head. On the other hand, when you swing outside-in, the club face comes at a steeper angle, giving less chance for grass to grab the club. Also, the open club face will add loft to help get the ball out.

Remember, generally the ball won't go as far. To hit a 9-iron distance from heavy rough, take the 7-iron. Just like with lay-ups on a par 5, if you can't get it to the green, pitch it to where you are most comfortable getting it to the green with your next shot.

The Absolutes of Golf

One, you have got to be *a good putter.*

Two, everything in golf is the moment of impact — getting the club to *hit the ball at the right time, in the right way.* There are different, even strange backswings and follow-throughs, but all that matters is that you get a square club face on the ball at impact.

Golf Strategy

Deciding When to Use a Fairway Wood

Calculate the risk-reward. If there is not too much trouble around the green, go ahead and hit it. When there is water and a lot of trouble around, it depends more on how you feel, and how you are hitting it that day. After all, if you lay up, you can still make birdie or a par with a wedge in your hand. Just because you can get there doesn't always mean you have to go for it.

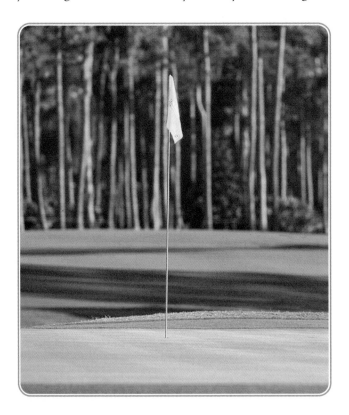

Keep Your Goals within Reason

Players sometimes get too concerned with a number and hurt themselves trying to reach it. For example, at the British Open at Birkdale, the 6th hole is a par 4, but into the wind, you can't get there in two. So against the field, a bogey is just like a par. And there are par 5s with the wind where par feels like a bogey.

Golf Is about Saving Strokes

Every time you save a stroke, you have accomplished something. Don't try to do things you haven't practiced when it might cost you one or two strokes.

Golf Strategy

Realistic Expectations

If a professional golfer puts a 2-iron around 30 feet from the pin, he or she has hit a pretty good shot. We might hit some shots within a couple of feet, but over the long haul, we don't expect to do much more with a 2-iron than put it around 14 yards, almost 45 feet.

Club players don't realize the average pro does hit his long irons like that — they just see us play on television, where the highlights show a guy hitting a 2-iron 10 feet from the hole. They don't see all the 2-irons we hit that miss the green, all the 2-irons we hit that leave us with a 40-foot putt.

Because of that, I think club players put too much pressure on themselves. If a club player hits a long iron onto the green, he ought to pat himself on the back.

The same, then, goes for fairway woods. At least 50 percent of my fairway woods miss the green.

Golf Strategy

Take Your Medicine When You Hit a Bad Shot

If you're in the rough or in the trees and can't do much, just lay it out to 100 yards, 80 yards, whatever is your favorite distance from the hole and make your next shot easier.

Golf Strategy

Patience in Golf

I've learned to be patient in golf because you never know how the round will end. There have been days where your worst start can turn out to be one of the best rounds you've ever played.

> *"If I do this for a living, yet go out there with the attitude that I should enjoy myself, then a club player should definitely make sure golf is fun."*

I shot 66 at the Masters once when nothing went right for the first three or four holes.

A "big picture" attitude helps you have patience because a round of golf is 18 holes, and a tournament is four days.

Find a Way to Be Relaxed

One of the keys to a big drive is *relaxation*. If you are tense, your muscles get shorter and tighter and you won't get the swing speed you need.

When I want to hit one hard, I know my tendency is to grit my teeth and white knuckle it. Those are the times I especially work on getting "loosey-goosey."

To get to that frame of mind, think about being oily or fluid. Another way to get loose is to picture someone like Fred Couples; this gives you a good image of someone who has a wonderful, fluid, and relaxed swing.

After all, brute force is not going to hit the ball a long way. It is club head speed that gets the ball out there, and the more relaxed you are, the more club head speed you generate.

When You Don't Go for the Green in Two

When you can't get to a par 5 in two, or you can't get close enough to the green to chip, lay up to a distance where you are comfortable hitting your next shot. Some players like to hit a 70-yard, 3/4 sand wedge. For me, I love to hit a full sand wedge 80 to 90 yards. Fifty yards from the green, I am not nearly as comfortable or as consistent as I will be from 80 or 90.

Take the Right Club

How do you know when you've got the right club? Don't judge your distance by your best shot, but judge it by your average shot. Too many times a club player will think, "Well, I've hit a 7-iron 150 yards before, so I'm going to hit it again," even though on average, they hit it only 140 yards.

As you select your club, decide where the best place is to miss the green. If there is a big bunker short of the green, and behind the green is a little grassy spot, take plenty of club and miss the bunker. Even if you hit too long, you are still in the safer spot.

Dealing with Pressure

I still get nervous, but my nervousness is because I want to do well. Even so, it is just a game. The most important thing in my life is my relationship with God and being the husband and father that He wants me to be. That has taken on a whole new meaning for me since I accepted Christ. The pressure is still there, but it is a totally different pressure than it was before because my satisfaction and security and significance are in Christ rather than in the results of my game — God loves me no matter what happens out there.

> *"What then shall we say to these things? If God is for us, who can be against us?"*
>
> ROMANS 8:31

Patience in Faith

In life some of the worst days turn out to be great days. And every day is a new day, though you are not guaranteed the next day. Knowing that God is sovereign, that He is in control of what happens to me, that God loves me, has patience with me, and forgives me, definitely helps me with my patience.

Life Strategy

Dedication and Golf

If you want to change your swing to get rid of a slice, and if you can work at it a couple of times a week, you will see some improvement in a month. To get rid of the slice completely, it may take longer. But you may always struggle with that outside-in swing to a degree. I have to fight being too inside-out, and I realize there will always be constant maintenance on my swing.

Faith takes that kind of dedication too. For example, there have been times when I have been tired and didn't want to go to the weekly Bible study while on Tour. Yet, I never leave the Bible study, not tickled that I went.

When you become a Christian, you are not going to lose all your vices overnight. God will help you — just like you can't expect to make a swing change overnight. It takes time, and you have got to be patient and dedicated.

In golf, like in life, if you are dedicated and committed, you will see results. Everybody who plays well in golf and excels has put in a lot of time, a lot of effort, and a lot of work.

So too, your faith; your relationship with God grows with the time and effort you put in. Jesus says those who knock and those who seek shall find. God wants us to ask, and He wants us to come to Him. Those who are dedicated and committed to Him continue to be rewarded by a closer and deeper relationship with Him. God will guide us if we seek him. You will have a peace and a joy that only God can give you. You may experience some heartaches and tough times, but you will still have a relationship with God that is indescribable. You will have a better life no matter what your circumstances.

But work and effort does not get you into Heaven. Only by God's grace can we spend eternity with Him.

Focus

Golf takes focus and discipline. You must work hard, and you must practice daily to play well.

And just like any relationship, a relationship with God requires discipline to be with Him every day.

In golf, I have to stay really focused when I am inside the ropes and not let anything distract me from performing to the best of my ability.

With God, distractions in the world will take your focus off of Him, especially when you get too busy to have time for God. That is my struggle; *I have got to make sure that I am not so busy* with everything that I am doing in golf that I don't sit down and open His word and read and pray with Him and have a devotion time.

Faith on the Tour

Players have said, "I respect what you believe, I respect your faith," although they might not agree with me. Those of us who are Christians on the Tour are not pushy in any way; we don't try to force anybody to come to our weekly Bible studies. We try to make an atmosphere at the study where nobody's called on, nobody is ever put on the spot, where people can just come, sit and listen, and leave when they want.

People like to ask, "Well, is it hard being a Christian on Tour?" I don't think it's any different than being a Christian anywhere else. It's just my workplace.

I've also heard the question, "Are you a better golfer because you are a Christian?" I can be a better golfer because of my faith. I have as much of a reason, or more of a reason now, to win golf tournaments and to glorify God. I want to show people that I can be successful and competitive and still have that personal relationship with Christ. And because of the eternal perspective I have, it helps me mentally in pressure situations.

Is the Tour easier as a Christian? The Tour can be lonely, and it can be tough out there. It helps when I know that I have fellow believers who are always there for me. I also know that I have God with me all the time. So from that standpoint, it is easier.

When I get back to the room, and I get a little lonely, I can always call my wife Bonnie anytime. We talk, and she helps. Our relationship is directly in line with Christ. As we get closer with Christ, and as the triangle grows, we get closer to each other. My most important relationship here on earth is with my wife.

Perspective

It is hard for us to realize — because we are finite beings — that our life here is nothing compared to eternity. When I think of eternity, I can't comprehend it; it doesn't end. This life is just a tiny little speck of sand in a huge, endless beach.

Yes, you have to be careful not to be so "heavenly minded that you are no earthly good," as the saying goes. But it is a comforting thought, when times get tough, that my hope is in Christ. He has made my life more abundant here, and I will have eternal life with Him forever. That gives me the hope in knowing that He is in charge and that everything will work out. It may not work out the way I want it to, but He knows a lot better than I do what is right, whether it is on the golf course or off.

When I lost the 1986 Tournament Players Championship, it may have been the best thing that ever happened to me; it may have helped me to win the Masters the next year. There are definitely some bad things that have happened to me in life, which turned out to be for good, but at the time I didn't know it.

I have comfort in knowing that God has revealed enough to us that we do know how the story ends. We do know it is going to be hard while we are here, but He is with us through it all.

FOCUS
Faith

Success

Success is using your God-given talent to the best of your abilities. It is not so much what you have accomplished as in what you have done with what you are given.

Winning the Masters

Winning the Masters taught me that no matter what I do in golf — Masters win, Ryder Cup Team, other tournament wins, overseas wins — those wins are not what make me significant. It is only from God's love for me through Jesus Christ that I am significant. Golf is fun and winning is great, but I am not significant because of them.

I need to continually remind myself of that. Because it is too easy to get caught up with what you do for a living, especially when it is going well — or just the opposite — you can get low when it is not going well.

Faith

What Victory Now Means

My golf has more meaning because I am trying to glorify God with it, rather than it glorifying me. Before it was: "I won, look at me, I am great." Now it is: "Hey, thanks, I appreciate it, but let me tell you of Someone who is great."

If I can't glorify God with a win, I don't want to win. It makes the win more satisfying and sweet because I am doing it for God, who loves me and who has done more for me than I deserve. All of life is better because of my relationship with Him.

Faith

Faith on the Golf Course

At the tournament at Hartford in 1998, with 4 holes to play, I had a 4-shot lead. I hit a shot to the right on 15 and made a double bogey. I missed a short putt, a 2 footer, on 16 for bogey. I lipped-out a putt on 17 for birdie and instead made par. Then I hit a good shot just over the green on 18, chipped it close, hit a good putt, and missed. *Making the putt would have won the tournament.*

Through it all, I was tempted to lose it, to really get mad, but I kept saying "No, stay calm, it's okay." While the specific thought of "playing for God" wasn't in my mind, the undercurrent of having Christ in my life let me know *"Larry, you're out here, you are representing Christ, and you need to keep your cool, trust in Him, and don't worry about it."*

To me, there is no doubt I would not have handled that very frustrating situation as well if it wasn't for my relationship with Christ. I was able to smile, applaud the guy who beat me in the play-off, and walk out of there with my head held high, because I had done the best that I could and I have a God who loves me and I am secure in that.

LIKE IT SAYS IN PHILIPPIANS 4:13,

I can do all things through Christ who strengthens me. It is not saying "I can do everything I want to do," but it is saying "I can handle everything that comes my way. My faith and the power He gives me help me to make the right choices and to keep things in perspective."

A Faith Lesson

Shortly after the 1986 TPC, I accepted Christ into my life. Before then, golf was the most important thing in my life. I found out that everything I had dreamed

of as a kid — the golf, the fame, the fortune, all that — wasn't going to give me everything I thought it would. I had every reason to be happy, and I was moping around because I only placed second at the TPC. I realized that I needed to have that personal relationship with Jesus Christ.

Flashback

Losing the Players Championship

Starting the final day at the The Players Championship in 1986, I had a 4-shot lead. On the 14th hole, I was still in first, with a 3-shot lead on John Mahaffey. The pin was on the right side of the green. I should have taken an 8-iron and put it right in the center of the green — which is what I would do today — and 2-putt. Inexperience hurt me. I thought I was playing so well I could go for it. Instead, I missed the green on the short side, and I made bogey.

On 15, John knocked it close. Again, inexperience hurt me. I figured if he knocked it close, I had better knock it close. I wasn't thinking that

par is good enough, that he must catch me. So again, I tried too hard, hit a bad shot, and made bogey.

Those two holes were keys to winning or losing the tournament. I went bogey, bogey and only lost one shot to him. Then there was a momentum swing, and I went on to bogey 16. I came back with a great shot on 17, then missed a short putt, and also bogeyed 18.

A 3-shot lead with four holes to play, tied with two holes to play, tied going into the last hole, and I lost it on the last hole. It was a tremendous disappointment. It is the 5th biggest tournament in the world, and I let it slip away.

The Masters at Augusta

On 18 of the final round, I knew I needed to make a birdie to tie.

Eighteen is a dogleg right, guarded at the turn by bunkers. Trees guard the right. Down the left are those two bunkers, reachable with a driver, and sometimes reachable with a 3-wood. You want to put the ball between the bunkers and the trees for the best angle into the pin.

Here was a situation where course management helped me. I was playing with Curtis Strange. I had a driver in my hand. Curtis teed off first and hit a 3-wood out to the right of the bunkers, a good distance. At that point, I thought it would be better not to chance the driver, so I put it back in the bag. I was able to hit a 3-wood in the fairway, leaving me a shot 140 yards uphill to the pin.

The pin was front left, another dicey position because the helping wind would take away spin. I knew that in a pressure situation, it is better to hit something hard rather than easy because *you help eliminate your nerves by being aggressive.* So I took a 9-iron and hit it hard, right at the pin. It landed 6 feet from the pin, went up the slope, but didn't get to the top of the ridge and rolled back down. It stopped about 6 feet away to leave me a right-edge putt, which I knocked in for my birdie to get into a play-off.

F(The)OCUS

Irons

Scott Simpson

When Scott Simpson won the 1998 Buick Invitational, his 8-stroke rally made it the single-largest comeback in almost 30 years of PGA golf. Yet golf fans might remember him more for another comeback — against Tom Watson at the 1987 U.S. Open Championship. One shot back at the beginning of the final round — facing the narrowed fairways, deepened rough, and treacherously fast greens that only the U.S. Open provides — Simpson used his strong iron play to birdie three of the last nine holes to edge Watson by a single stroke.

With seven PGA tour wins, Simpson almost won his second U.S. Open in 1991, losing an 18-hole play-off to Payne Stewart. With Ryder Cup and Walker Cup experience, Simpson has finished as high as 4th on the PGA money list, and as his recent Buick Invitational win proves, is a threat no matter how tough the competition.

Much as he is accustomed to victory, Scott finds satisfaction looking beyond the trophies and fame. Stand beside him as he helps you swing your irons better, and focus with him on golf and more . . .

The Takeaway

Make sure your hips turn at the beginning of your takeaway. Your arms, wrists, and club move back together — something you can't do if your muscles and grip are tight. Relax, make a good turn, and let the club swing instead of trying to overcontrol with just your hands and arms.

With this takeaway, you start the downswing with your body, let the club head lag behind, and get pulled down into the ball. This ensures — especially with a long iron which tends to sweep — that you hit down on the ball and take a divot. If you hit down, you'll put spin on the ball, and it will rise.

FOCUS

The Swing

The Backswing

On the backswing, make a good turn with your shoulders. Don't just lift the club with your hands and arms, because on the downswing the club will come from the outside and you will slice the ball.

If you want the club to swing down at the ball from the inside instead of the outside, your left shoulder must turn and get over your right knee. As your shoulders turn back, your right hip is turning behind you, moving away from the ball. A good turn back like this will let you get the club behind you as you begin to swing down. When the club lags behind your body on the downswing, it will drop to the inside so that you swing from inside to out, eliminating a slice.

The Downswing

At the top of your backswing, you must be set with your weight on your right side, left heel perhaps a little off the ground. Your hips are turned about 40 degrees and your shoulders turned close to 90 degrees. The club is behind you, and you are ready to go.

This is similiar to how a quarterback gets on his right foot to allow himself to push off and throw. Or like a baseball pitcher who is ready to push off the rubber and stride with his left leg.

From this position in golf, your downswing begins as your weight moves from the inside of your right foot over to the left foot. At the same time, your hips turn and are pulling your hands and arms down. The club will naturally release this energy into and through the ball. You don't want to get the hands moving too quickly at the start of the downswing. Avoid "casting" — getting the club head ahead of your hands in the way that you cast a fishing rod. This forces the club head to the outside, and it will cut across the ball on the way down, resulting in a weak slice. Remember, instead, to make it the opposite of a "cast." Your body moves to the left, turns out of the way, and then the hands and arms follow and release through the ball.

With this move, you've got to move laterally a little. With the best players, their hips will move about 6 inches left on the downswing. But the difference is that they are also turning as they move left.

If you only move left, and slide with no hip turn, then your body stops and your hands flip at the ball, which results in a big duck hook. If you only turn your hips and don't move laterally, you end up swinging off your right foot, and you will cut across the ball.

The Swing

Adding Backspin

You can't hit a shot with spin unless you use a ball that will spin.

With the right ball, you generate spin the same way it happens in pool or tennis. In pool, you hit down on the cue ball to get it to come back at you; in tennis, to hit a drop shot, you chop down on the back of the ball.

In golf, too, you've got to hit down on the back of the ball. You've got to hit the ball first and take a divot after the ball. If you hit behind the ball at all, you will lose spin because grass gets between the ball and the club. So think of pinching the ball between the ground and the club head, almost as if you are using the face of the club to compress the ball into the ground.

Place the ball just behind your left heel in your stance. As you hit, the club head must be trailing your hands so that your hands are ahead of the ball as the club head hits it, still moving on a downward arc.

Another key is to make sure you don't flip at the ball with your hands. Never try to help the ball up in the air because as soon as you do that, the club head is past your hands at impact, which means the club head is coming up instead of hitting down.

Spin is important with the short irons, especially if you are hitting over bunkers, water, and any kind of trouble where you will need to stop the ball quickly.

Hit Down to Drive the Ball Up

Players find it more difficult to hit longer irons because they look down and see clubs without much loft and think they're not going to be able to hit the shot into the air. But if you feel you need to "help the ball up," you will stay back on your right side and flip your wrists upward. You'll either top the ball or hit the ground first.

When you start to top it every time, invariably your partner will say that you lifted your head. That's not the problem. You need to relax, transfer the weight from your right side to your left side, and hit down on the ball. That will give your shot the backspin that is going to make the ball go up into the air.

The driver is about the only club where you don't hit down on the ball, simply because it's already teed up. Because the driver is the longest club, the swing is more of a sweep, with the ball forward in your stance a bit. But with an iron, even a long iron, you still want to hit down on the ball.

Long Irons versus Mid Irons

Your goal should be to make the same swing with every club, to use the same swing thought. Because a middle iron and a long iron are not a lot different, you don't need to try to do anything differently.

Because the long iron tends to be more of a sweeping swing, you do need a good lie. With a middle iron you will hit down on the ball more, but that is not generated by a change in your swing. It is generated by the loft and the arc of the shorter club. When the club is shorter, and the ball closer to you, your swing is a little more upright than with a long iron.

As for any change in stance, play most of your shots with the ball off the left heel, a little bit forward in your stance. This will help you because it makes you move to your left side as you hit the ball. When the ball is back in your stance, you may get away with just slapping at it with your hands and arms because you don't have to move your body to reach it.

Shotmaking

Ball above the Feet

When the ball is above your feet, take an extra club and choke up on it. Play for a little draw. If the ball is really above your feet, use less leg drive and swing from the shoulders because the tendency otherwise is for the club to hit the ground behind the ball.

Shotmaking

Ball below the Feet

When the ball is below your feet, bend your knees slightly more than usual and play for a fade. Also, move the ball closer to your stance; you want your arms to just hang over the ball. In general, you never want to be reaching for the ball — that adds tension to your arms.

A Downhill Lie

With a downhill lie, with your normal swing, the tendency is to catch the top of the ball. To counteract this, angle your shoulders to match the slope you're standing on. Put more weight on your left side, and it will lower your left shoulder. By doing this, your regular swing will allow you to hit down on the ball and still take a divot. The golf swing is difficult enough; you want to be able to hit different shots with the same swing.

Lastly, put the ball a bit back in your stance and play for a fade.

In terms of club selection, it depends on the wind and what the ball has to carry. With a downhill lie, the shot is going to fly lower, and it's going to roll. If you do have room to play for that roll, it will probably require the same club for distance that you would use on a regular lie.

Shotmaking

An Uphill Lie

An uphill lie, of course, is the exact opposite of the downhill lie. The tendency on an uphill shot is to drive the club into the ground. So you want to lower your right shoulder to get your body tilted with the slope of the ground.

Make a normal swing, still hitting down on the ball. Take an extra club because it is going to fly higher than normal.

Long Irons out of the Rough

A shot from the rough depends on the thickness of the rough. At a course like the U.S. Open, where the rough is grown high, your main goal is to get the ball back to the fairway. Once you get the ball out, you normally only have another short iron left to the green, and you still have a shot at making par. From thick rough, drop to a short iron to give you something that can cut through the grass and still get the ball up in the air.

As the rough gets a bit lower, you can reach the green. The trouble there is that you might hit a "flier." This happens when grass gets between the ball and the club, and the ball comes out like a spitter in baseball. It has no spin on it and could go any direction. Also it's going to fly farther because it doesn't have any backspin. And when it lands, it's going to roll a long way.

In this situation, I'll often take one or two less club. Where I might hit a 6-iron from the fairway, I will hit an 8-iron from the rough. Hopefully I'll have room to land it on the front edge and let it roll up by the hole. But my expectations will be to try to get it onto the green first and then try to get it close to the hole.

From the rough, you definitely need to lower your expectations. Often I see players in pro-ams, on the difficult courses we play, who try to hit long irons out of the rough, and the ball goes about three feet.

Shotmaking

Irons into the Wind

To play a shot into the wind, put the ball back in your stance and shorten your swing. Make certain that your hands are leading the club head through the impact area.

You want the club to come through with a shallow arc as it hits the ball. Hitting steeply down on the ball will add spin, and the more spin on the ball, the more it's going to shoot up in the air against the wind.

For that reason, you need to use more club, maybe an extra two or three depending on the wind. A 7-iron with no wind might become a 4-iron so that you can put it back in your stance and take a smooth swing. An easy swing with less loft reduces spin, and the ball will hold its line better and not rise into the wind.

Low Shots and High Shots

To hit a low shot, the key is to change your address position. Put the ball back in your stance, and take a shorter swing so that your hands lead the club head through impact, which takes loft off the club.

To hit a high shot — hitting over a tree, for example — put the ball up in your stance. This gets your right shoulder lower as you set up. This again means you can make your regular swing, but because the ball is farther ahead, the club head will be even with your hands during impact. It will be more of a sweeping swing, and because the club effectively has more loft on it, the ball will rise higher.

Hooking and Slicing on Cue

To hit a fade or a hook *without changing your swing, change your setup.*

If you need to fade it around a tree, aim the club face where you want the ball to end up, but aim your body left on the line where you want the ball to start. This will get you to swing across your line, without changing your swing. The ball will start left according to your swing path, but because the club face is open, a left-to-right spin will move the ball to the right.

To hook the ball, of course, do the opposite. This way, you can hit a lot of different shots by changing your setup instead of changing your swing.

Avoid Preshot Fear

One of the keys to hitting a good long iron is to stay relaxed.

This will allow you to make a good full turn on the backswing. A lot of players — especially when they're afraid they might hit a bad shot — tend to tense up. Not only don't they make a good turn, but they rush into the downswing, with bad results.

In a pressure situation your tendency is to grip the club harder. When you grip it too hard, it shortens your swing, your swing ends up being all hands and arms, and again, you don't make a good turn with your body.

I like Sam Snead's analogy about gripping the club the same way you would a bird in your hand. Not hard enough to squeeze the life out of it, but hard enough so that the bird won't get away.

You want your forearms to be relaxed. Grip it hard enough so the club's not going to fly out of your hands, which I've never seen happen. But I've sure seen the opposite side where a player has got a death grip and I can see white knuckles because the fingers are wrapped so tightly around the club.

Focus

In golf, the best way to focus is for brief periods of time. Don't grind for five hours in a row. You can't do it. You wear yourself out mentally. Relax in between the shots; give yourself some time off.

The Absolutes of Golf

P*utt well. That's how you win tournaments.*

Practice to be consistent. (No one is going to hit every shot perfect. Otherwise guys would be shooting in the 40s.) That is why you need to work hard to *get a swing that is going to repeat itself* and be consistent, so that even if you miss the ball a bit — a little behind, or a little thin — it will still go relatively straight and relatively the same distance.

Even if your misses always tend to fade, or draw, you can work with that. But if you never know how far the ball will go, or you don't know whether it will hook or slice, you'll have a difficult play.

Golf Strategy

Choosing Long Irons over Fairway Woods

When hitting a long iron you must hit the ball solidly, or it may be an ugly shot. A fairway wood gives a larger margin for error, and because of that, lofted woods are more popular.

But the loft of a fairway wood tends to put the ball up in the air and allow it to hook and slice more. A long iron tends to go straighter. If you want to be a better player, if you want to improve your game, you need to learn to hit your long irons.

Golf Strategy

How to Relax

> *"Relaxation is the number one key to a good swing."*

Relaxation is absolutely *the number one key to a good swing*. I want to make the same swing on the golf course that I make on the practice range. I need to relax and stick with my routine, which is, for me, a practice swing, two waggles, and then hit it.

This is easy to say, but hard to do, and it takes some practice to find your own routine.

Physically, I take a deep breath and slow down. Mentally, I don't think about the outcome, only the process of hitting the shot.

I think that is where *my faith helps* because I don't need to worry about being embarrassed. If I am giving it my best — even if my game stinks that day — and keep the right attitude, I'm performing for Christ, the way He would want me to. There is satisfaction in that, even if my performance isn't my best.

FOCUS
Golf Strategy

Expectations

You will take birdies with long or middle irons when you can get them, but your main goal should simply be to get them on the green. Wait until you're hitting short irons to expect to get the ball close to the hole.

Golf Strategy

Pressure

It is important to have the same physical routine for each shot. Whether it is Tuesday on the practice tee or Sunday afternoon on the last tee at the U.S. Open, you want to make the same swing. A repeating routine will give you the same frame of mind for both.

First, *go through a mental routine*. Focus on your shot and analyze what you want to do with it.

The 18th hole at Bay Hill has one of the scariest second shots we have on Tour. When I stand over that shot, I want to know where the water is, where the bunkers are, where all the trouble is. And I want to know how I am playing that day, whether I am feeling confident or not. Do I shoot at the pin, or do I play it safe? Do I take an extra club? All of these variables enter into my shot decision.

When it is time to focus on your shot, forget about all the trouble. Pick out your target and visualize your shot going there. Take your practice swing, and feel the swing that will make the right shot when you set up over the ball. Then, make the same swing as the practice swing.

Afterward, whether you hit a good shot or bad, analyze it. "I was a little quick on that" or "I didn't quite make a good turn," or "Man, that felt good." *Analyze your shot, then let it go and relax* as you go down the fairway until you reach your next shot.

Golf Strategy

Deciding whether a Situation Needs a Long Iron or Fairway Wood

Choosing a long iron or fairway wood depends on your lie. From a good lie, an iron is easier to hit because it will go straighter. If you hit the fairway wood well, the ball will have more spin on it than one hit by a long iron, so it will stop quicker.

Trajectory is another reason to choose a long iron. If there is any wind, the shot's lower trajectory will get the ball to cut through the wind better, giving better distance control. A lofted fairway wood, which is going to rise quicker and higher in the air, will be at the mercy of the wind.

Because of this, a lot of times Tour players will take a one-iron to the British Open, even if we don't use it much during the year. At the Masters, where it's not usually windy, we carry water to the greens on the back nine par 5s, and a lot of us will take 4- or 5-woods when we normally wouldn't use those.

So, *choosing long irons over woods often depends on the course and the conditions.*

Golf Strategy

What Kind of Ball Works for You

If you use a "harder" ball — a surlyn — the cover won't cut if you hit it thin. It will curve less, compared to the softer balata balls, which most of the pros use. Balata balls spin more, and for a higher handicap player, this softer ball will magnify any mistakes in hooking or slicing.

Surlyn-covered "distance" balls go 5 to 8 yards farther than a balata ball off the tee. If the fairway is hard and dry, they may go up to 15 yards farther because of the bounce and roll. Also, the "distance" balls are comparatively a lot longer with irons than with drivers. A 5-iron distance ball might go 10 yards farther because of the relative lack of spin.

Just remember there is a trade-off. Because of the softer covers and extra spin, *balata balls stop better* and *give you an advantage* with short irons and chip shots around the greens.

Right Choices on the Course

In golf, the secret is to get a swing that repeats so that your mishits go straight and leave you with a playable shot. With that kind of swing, you won't go out of bounds, and you can manage your way around hazards and not make the double and triple bogeys that can ruin your round.

What to Do When Between Clubs

Don't overswing on any iron. If you are between an 8- and 9-iron shot, choose the 8 and make an easier swing. Don't choke down on the 8-iron to reduce the arc of the swing to a 9-iron; the easier swing will give you better tempo and more control over your shot.

Make sure you don't decelerate, however, as you swing easier. You definitely want to hit through every shot to a good, full finish.

The Absolutes in **Golf** & Life

To play your best golf, *you need to be having fun.* Even for the pros, who are working hard and concentrating on each shot, it shouldn't be a grind. I have always played my best when I'm not grinding and trying too hard and putting a lot of pressure on myself — telling myself I have to make this par, or I have to make this putt to win this tournament. When I am enjoying myself and letting it happen, I play to my ability.

In the same way, *no one should have more fun than a Christian.* We should always be ready to put a smile on our faces. We can have a joyful and abundant life; after all, *we have an eternity to look forward to that is far better than anything we have on earth.*

The Absolutes in **Life** & Golf

One of the *most important things* is to *be honest.*

In golf, I need to be honest with myself. If, for example, on the course that day most of my shots are fading, I've got to play with that even if I want to hit a draw. If I'm not hitting the ball as far, I'll need to take a 7-iron where I might usually hit an 8-iron.

In the same way, you need to *be honest dealing with everybody around you.* Life is a lot easier that way because then you have nothing to hide. You don't always have to think about covering up your lies.

Focus

I had won earlier in the year at Greensboro, but the week before the 1987 U.S. Open at Westchester, I was frustrated with my game. I felt like I was hitting it okay, but I wasn't scoring well. I was getting mad, banging clubs, and saying a few things I shouldn't, which made me even madder at myself.

On Wednesday, the week of the U.S. Open, our Bible study subject focused on how true contentment comes from Jesus Christ. We know we will be with Him forever and that there are things more important than anything we will do in this life. I refocused on how *contentment doesn't come from where you stand on the money list or whether you win or lose*. What I did that week in Bible study was write down Colossians 3:17.

> *"And whatever you do in word or deed, do all in the name of the Lord Jesus, giving thanks to God the Father through Him."*
> COLOSSIANS 3:17

Instead of worrying about winning, or coming in the top 15 and making the Masters, or making the cut, or all those things, I filled my mind with Christ. I wanted to please Him by just giving it my best and remember how fortunate I was to even be one of the guys playing.

FOCUS
Life Strategy

Self-Worth

There is no doubt that *sometimes things don't go very well*. But good things *can* come from tragedy. My friend, Dave Dravecky, was on top of the world and pitched in the World Series. A few years later he didn't even have his pitching arm. But he lives with joy and abundance, helping other amputees, cancer victims, and their families through a great ministry, the "Outreach of Hope." It would be a lot more difficult for him if he thought his self-worth was based only on his ability as a baseball pitcher.

Life Strategy

Making the
Right Choices

God's commandments are there for us to get the most out of life. When I bought my laptop computer, I read the instruction manual to learn how to operate it correctly, rather than just banging keys and not knowing what I am doing.

Through the Bible, God gives us an instructional manual for how to get the most out of life. Avoid some things, do other things, and, as Paul says, you will have an abundant, joyful, happy life no matter what your circumstances.

> *"Delight yourself also in the LORD, and He shall give you the desires of your heart. Commit your way to the LORD, trust also in Him, and He shall bring it to pass."*
>
> PSALM 37:4,5

Life is basically a series of choices. There is a downside to sin. Sin may feel good in the short run, but in the long-term, it leads to emptiness. God made us to work best when we do what is good, what is right, and what is honorable. When you follow Him, it might not appear to be as much fun in the short run — but the payoff is down the road in a joyful, happy, and fulfilling life.

FOCUS

Winning the U.S. Open:
A Faith Lesson

I finished 1987 at number 4 on the money list, which is the highest I have ever finished. I was looking forward to 1988, thinking it would be bigger and better than ever. Instead, I had my worst finish ever on the money list.

In hindsight, part of it was being too busy being the U.S. Open Champion. Everyone wanted me to do something. I traveled and played in a lot of different tournaments and places, and it wore me out. I didn't practice as much. And the pressure of trying to live up to being the U.S. Champion was tough.

> *"Rejoice always, pray without ceasing, in everything give thanks; for this is the will of God in Christ Jesus for you."*
> I THESSALONIANS 5:16-18

It became a vicious spiral because the worse I played, the more pressure I put on myself. When I didn't play well, I started trying to change things.

I remember the Masters, missing the cut in 1988, which was the fourth cut in a row I'd missed. My whole family was out there. My brother was caddying, and I really wanted to play well. I was dejected, but at the same time it reminded me again of where my true contentment came from.

Finding Faith

I met my wife Cheryl in high school. She was a Christian, and I wasn't. For me at that time, Christianity was strictly a psychological crutch — opium of the masses, something to keep people in line. I didn't believe any of it and was dead-set against it. But, I was interested in Cheryl, so I would question her about it. She was not a real Bible scholar, and after a while, we didn't talk much about it because she couldn't answer my questions.

When I got on tour, one week in 1980, I went to a Bible study. It was on Psalm 23 — The Lord is my Shepherd — about us being the sheep and not being able to take care of ourselves without a Shepherd. I thought, "Who would want to go through life being a sheep? Not me! I don't need anyone protecting me. I'm going to make it on my own."

In 1981, I went to an open discussion group with a fellow named Larry Moody, whose background is in apologetics. For the first time, I was able to ask my questions about God and life, and Larry gave me answers that made sense. He didn't put me down for having a different opinion.

He did challenge me the first night with questions of his own.

Who was Jesus? What did he say? The claims about Him were either true or false. I read Josh McDowell's *More Than A Carpenter,* a book where Josh began by trying to prove Christianity wrong only to see it proved right.

When, intellectually, all my questions had been answered, it was just a matter of giving up my pride and saying, "Christ, I do need you." I faced the fact I wasn't perfect and that I did need Christ so that I could be in Heaven for all time.

Faith Sustains

In the 1991 U.S. Open, we played at Hazeltine Country Club, in Minneapolis, Minn. Payne Stewart and I were neck and neck for the championship, and no one else was even close. I had him by two with three holes to go. I ended up bogey-ing 16 and 18 and went to a play-off the next day.

In the play-off we went back and forth, and again, I was two-up with three to go. On 16 this time, I hit it in the middle of the fairway and hit a good shot to the middle of the green. Payne was about the same place. I ended up leaving my putt about 3 feet short; he knocked it in from 25 feet. I missed my little putt and now we were even with two holes to go.

He hit a good shot on 17, a par 3 about 185 yards with a big lake on the left. I hit a terrible shot and pulled it into the water. At that point, I didn't give up, but I knew,

barring a miracle, I had just blown the U.S. Open.

Still, there were two holes left. I was able to regroup; I dropped the ball on the other side of the hazard, hit a great shot to about 10 feet, and made it for bogey. Payne missed his 8-footer for birdie and made par, so I was only one down.

> *"A good name is to be chosen rather than great riches, loving favor rather than silver and gold."*
> PROVERBS 22:1

I ended up losing on the last hole. Losing, when I had been leading twice, was tough.

Obviously I wasn't happy with finishing badly, but at the same time, I was able to know it's not the end of the world, and there are things more important — like my faith and my family.

Faith

Faith on the Tour

My perspective has changed since putting my faith in Christ. I am thankful for what I have. Through my deeds, I desire to do the very best I can; through my words, to give Him the glory.

People sometimes ask whether Christ helps us win tournaments, as if Christianity is a psychological crutch. That's not the way it is. He helps us whether we win or lose.

In that respect, *if your perspective is right*, He is going to help you to do your best, whether you are a janitor or a teacher or a pro golfer.

He helped me to have the right attitude the week I won the U.S. Open. I was very relaxed as I played. When I went into the press room afterwards on Sunday, members of the press asked, "Scott you've never won a major before, you beat Tom Watson by one shot . . . yet we saw you smiling out there, and you seemed relaxed. How did you do that?"

I shared about where true contentment came from. I think half of them were looking away like, "Oh, not another guy trying to push his religion on me." The other half were interested in what I was *talking about*, in how faith could help them.

I will not try to push my faith on anyone. Trust in Christ is a personal decision, between each one of us and God.

I love to be able to share my faith, however, because trusting in Christ is the most important thing any of us can do in our lives. The cure for sin is more important than the cure for AIDS, or cancer, or anything else.

> *Trusting in Christ is the most important thing any of us can do in our lives.*

FOCUS
Flashback

On Golf

It's a crazy game. You miss the cut one week, and win the next. I don't know why it happens that way. You try to play so that your misses go straight to give you pars and occasional bogies, knowing your good shots will go close for some birdies. When that happens on tour, you will do well.

Winning the U.S. Open

It was at the Olympic Club, San Francisco — a great golf course. Only one fairway bunker on the whole course, no water, not that long either, and yet it is an unbelievable challenge.

Much of the challenge was the rough, a good 5-inches deep. If you missed the fairway, you would most often just try to get back to the fairway instead of trying to reach the green.

Also, the fairways tend to have doglegs out where you want to hit your drives. A good drive might land in the fairway and roll right through into the rough. On a lot of holes you hit a 3-wood off the tee to keep it in the area where the fairway bends.

I was one shot back going into the last day. Tom Watson and Keith Clearwater were leading. They were two under, and I was one under — I played with Lenny Clements, who was also one under. There were a bunch of guys at even par. At that point, a double- or triple-bogey can take you right off the leader board, but at the same time, a couple of birdies can get you back in there.

It looked like even par was going to be a great score. All week the course had been tough, and the last day the greens continued to get firm and were tough to putt. In fact, on Saturday I played really well tee-to-green and was frustrated with my putting. I had been hitting it 10 to 15 feet from the pin all day and couldn't make any birdies. I finally made a putt on the last hole for a birdie to get to one-under going into Sunday's round. I was still frustrated, and practiced my putting for about an hour Saturday night.

I was definitely nervous that day, being near the lead. At the same time, I was relaxed, knowing I was going to do my best, not worry about the

> "A man's heart plans his way, but the Lord directs his steps."
> PROVERBS 16:9

results, and just think about the shots I was hitting. I made a commitment not to look at the leader board, but to play my game and concentrate on making good shots.

To start the final round, I made a 20-foot putt on the first hole — for birdie — a downhill, sidehill putt to jump into the lead.

Then I made bogeys on holes 3, 4, and 6. They are tough holes, but at the same time, to make those bogeys was not fun. Then I ended up birdying hole 7 from about 8 feet and made the turn after nine holes at one over par for the day, and par for the tournament. It looked like even par might have a chance to win.

At that point I was one shot behind Watson, who was making the turn. I carried on and made pars, and at the 14th hole hit a 7-iron to about 6 feet and made it for birdie to put me one under for the tournament. On the next hole I hit an 8-iron to the middle of the green, a safe shot, leaving me a putt uphill through the shadows. I was just trying to lag it, but I knocked it in from about 25 feet for another birdie.

When I got to 16, my first thought was of 1965 when Arnold Palmer hit a duck hook off the tee there and even with a miraculous bogey ended up losing the U.S. Open. I overcompensated and hit my drive into the rough on the right side. I was fortunate to get a decent lie under a tree where the gallery had trampled it down. I hit a 2-iron out of there, and it rolled up the fairway. I hit a 9-iron onto the green about 15 feet and made that one for birdie. It put me three under, and I began to think I might have a good lead.

Finally, I looked at the leader board and saw that Watson had also birdied 14, and he was two under with everybody else over par. So with two holes to go, I knew it was going to be a great week with me being either first or second in the U.S. Open, but I really wanted to win.

I knew there was a lot of golf to go over those last two holes, and I was able to refocus.

Hole 17 is a long par four uphill, a par five for the members. I hit a good drive, but it kicked just into the short rough. I hit it up into the left bunker. Most people remember the bunker shot as being some miraculous shot, but I didn't think it was as difficult as most people remember. I had a lot of green to work with, and I blasted about 8 feet past the hole and made that putt for par. I had just made 4 great one-putts in a row, and it seemed like all the putts I had missed the day before were now going in.

On 18, the pin was in the middle, so I hit a good 2-iron off of the tee. It's an uphill hole, and I knew I didn't want to hit my second shot past the pin because it would be a real difficult putt coming back down the hill. I followed my 2-iron with a good 8-iron about 15 feet to the right, just under the hole. From there, I wanted to make sure I two-putted. I lagged it 6 inches short of the hole and knocked it in, then waited around to see what Watson was going to do.

Watson made pars on 16 and 17. That meant he needed to birdie 18 to force a play-off. He hit a 9-iron that landed on the front of the green and spun back to the fringe. I thought there was no way he would make that putt, 40 feet uphill, right-to-left, with the the greens bumpy at the end of the day.

I was watching that putt on the television monitor behind the 18th green, and the closer it got to the hole, the better it looked. I really didn't want to play Watson in an 18-hole play-off the next day. He is from Stanford, a local hero and an all-time great golfer. But the putt missed by about 1/4 of an inch.

He was unbelievably gracious in defeat, which was the same way Nicklaus had been to him when he beat Nicklaus all those times. I know that it hurt him a lot to lose there, where he went to school and on a course that he loved, but he lost the same way he won, as a champion with class.

It was a dream come true for me — literally. Growing up, my golfing heroes were Nelson and Hogan and Nicklaus and Jones, all these guys who had won the U.S. Open. So it was the ultimate win for me.

F(The)CUS
Short Game
Loren Roberts

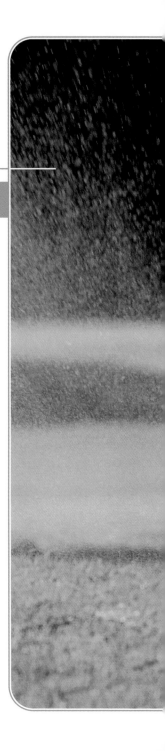

How well does Loren Roberts putt? How good is his short game? Sandwiched among the superstars of two generations — with Jack Nicklaus and Lee Trevino on one side and Tiger Woods and David Duval on the other — fellow PGA Tour players have an insider nickname for him: "Boss of The Moss."

In 1994, Loren's first PGA Tour victory came at a tournament that intimidates even the best players, Arnold Palmer's Bay Hill Invitational. Then Loren repeated by winning the next year, becoming the only player to successfully defend at Bay Hill. At his MCI Classic victory, he broke Hale Irwin's tournament record.

Against the field of today's incredible talent, Loren is one of the few modern players to consistently win tournaments from year to year. In fact, cracked ribs forced him out of play early in 1998, yet he finished the season by making 13 consecutive cuts and finished in the top 10 an amazing three times.

A President's Cup and Ryder Cup player, Loren Roberts understands golf as well as any player on Tour. And he understands something more. Share some time with him in golf and learn how to *focus on what really matters on and off the course* . . .

Controlling the Length and Speed of Your Putt

With a pendulum putting stroke, the speed of your putt is controlled by the length of your back stroke. Longer, of course, equates to farther. With practice, you will learn how to judge your distance. Keep in mind this works the same for chipping and pitching the ball around the greens. You'll be amazed at how easy it is once you learn it.

"Breaking" the Wrist

If you are having trouble with speed control, check your hand action during your putting stroke, especially on longer putts. You *don't* want to hold a stiff-wristed grip past your right hip on the takeaway. Because if you don't have any wrist break, you haven't set the club in a position where you can hit it with any force. While this is more prominent in the chipping and pitching motion, with the putter you still need a little bit of that wrist cock on the takeaway. Where it is crucial to *keep* the wrist stiff is on the follow-through.

The Putting Stroke

The perfect putting stroke is a pure pendulum action — the back stroke and the follow-through should be the same distance on either side of the ball. This takes the "hit" out of a putting stroke because when you have a shorter back stroke than follow-through, you have to "hit" at the ball, and this tends to push or pull it off-line. Instead, for a steadier roll, just let the ball get in the way of the pendulum swing.

To practice, take a yard stick onto the putting green to make sure that when you take it back 12 inches, for example, your follow-through is 12 inches. Learn this feeling.

Hit Every Putt
18 Inches Past the Hole?

When I'm shooting baskets and I'm trying to make a free throw, I don't bank it hard off the backboard. I want the basketball to go up and in.

While I don't really want a putt to fall in the hole on the last roll, the right speed is any speed that allows you to get the ball up around the hole and in. After all, if you're good enough from 40 feet to hit it past the hole 18 inches, why not just knock it in?

The Stroke

Stance and Grip

Stand as tall as you comfortably can over a putt. Don't hunch over, elbows sticking out. The more you get down, the tougher it is for you to see the line of the putt.

And when you stand as tall as you can, your arms are going to hang naturally. This makes it easier to get the right putting grip. With a regular golf swing, you want your palms together on a normal grip, but when you putt, you want your palms opposed as much as you can. When you oppose your palms, it pulls in your elbows, so that your forearms are on the same plane — you don't have one elbow out and one in.

Think of it this way: if someone handed you a heavy tray, and you were to hold it up, your forearms would be together on the same plane or the tray would tip. You want this feeling when you putt, so that your arms and shoulders are working together.

The Absolute Key
to Good Putting

Speed is the key to putting. *Proper line* is secondary.

Most players approach it in the opposite way. They worry about the line so much that they forget about the speed. Even a 3- to 5-foot putt can be on the perfect line, but at the wrong speed, it is not going to go in.

Not only that, but most putts have a little bit of bend. A ball at the right speed doesn't have to be dead center to go in the hole. After all, the ball is a lot smaller than the hole — at the right speed it can go in from four directions. A putt can even come in from behind if it rolls around the edge of the cup.

Say you have to make a 3- to 5-foot putt for the club championship in your home club — the last thing you want to worry about is trying to hit the perfect line to make it go in the center of the cup. Because from 3 to 5 feet, you're pretty much always going to be on the right line. If you just worry about controlling the speed, it takes the pressure off of "aiming" a putt. Think of it this way: the worst thing a pitcher can do when he starts losing control is to try to aim the ball.

Speed is even more important on longer putts. When I play in the pro-ams on the Wednesdays of a tournament, I never see amateurs off-line more than 2 feet on putts from 25 to 30 feet. Yet I've seen them leave it 15 feet short or knock it 15 feet past. If your speed is right, you will always get it close to the hole and cut down on 3-putts.

The Dreaded 40- or 50-yard Chip

The key to a 40- or 50-yard chip is to set the angle of the wrists on the backswing and then turn your shoulders through on the downswing and follow-through. Most people think, "I've got to hit it with my hands." Instead, hit with your shoulder turn. That way, the length of the backswing determines how far the ball is going to go, not the force of that perfect touch you've got to have with the hands at the bottom of the swing.

*"I remember getting to the press room after I had won —
one of the questions was: 'It took you 11 years on the Tour
before you finally won. Why didn't you just quit?'*

*Up to that point I'd had the distinction of having won
the most official money on Tour without having won. So, it
wasn't like I was going broke out there; it was a good living."*

Shotmaking

Greenside Bunkers

Contrary to what a lot of people think, sometimes the bunker shot is the easiest shot in golf. Once you learn the idea and the technique behind the bunker shot, all you need to do is adjust to the different sand textures. In Florida, for example, you have really powdery sand; up north, you have gravelly, grainy sand.

The idea behind the shot is that you never ever hit the ball. Treat it as if it were an extra large grain of sand on top of a pile of sand that you are going slice beneath and throw out of the bunker. To do this, slide the club 2 or 3 inches behind and under the ball as you swing through.

With a bunker shot, you still want to use shoulder swing instead of trying to judge the distance with your hands. The more shoulders you use, the more you set the angle of the wrists on the backswing. As you carry your shoulders on through, the hands will go the same speed as the shoulder turn.

FOCUS
Shotmaking

Loren's Focus Key

With chipping and pitching shots, I focus on the spot on the green where I want the ball to land in order for it to stop around the hole. Once I've decided where that spot is, my shoulder rotation stroke allows me to get the ball to that spot with consistent spin and roll on the ball. Remember, speed control is very important with chipping, pitching, and putting.

Shotmaking

The High Soft Lob Shot

With this shot, you are trying to hit the ball higher than the club is designed for. It means you have to make adjustments. Open your stance and aim more left, which also opens the club face to compensate; the more you aim your body left, the more the club face will open if you continue to aim at the target.

This means when you swing the club back, it goes outside, so essentially you are swinging as if you are trying to hit a big slice. Swing down and through, and on this shot you want the right hand to release. Once you get through the ball, let the hand release under it.

This shot must be constantly practiced — you involve many moving parts of your hands and arms and shoulders as you manipulate the club to do something that it is not particularly designed for.

The 60-degree wedge is useful if you have trouble getting the ball airborne around the green. Basically it is the sand wedge with 4 or 5 degrees more loft. Again, you have to spend a little more time practicing with this club because the more loft, the more of a glancing blow you actually place on the ball.

The Running Pitch

The pitch and run is much like a long putt. From off the green, the chip shot is in the air for a short period, then it runs as much as possible along the surface of the green.

Just like with a putt, stand as tall as you can. You may want to open your stance a little bit, but it is the same pendulum action as a putt.

A real *key focus is consistency*. If you cock the angle of the wrists on the backswing, and think "shoulders through," the left hand never flips or breaks down on impact, and your hands will move through the shot at the same speed as your shoulder turn. Again, this takes the "hit" out of the shot with your hands. This way you will always be able to consistently judge your distances.

Golf Strategy

The Absolutes
of Good Golf

If you can learn two things in the game, you can be a really consistent player. Learn to drive the ball in the fairway — from there, you can nearly always get it up somewhere around the green, if not on the green. Second, learn a good short game — because if you are near the green, you can always get the ball in position close to the hole.

To be a good player on any level, follow this general rule: always give yourself a putt for par. Never play such a marginal shot that it will take you out of the possibility of a putt for par. For example, if you have to hook it around a tree and over a lake to get it back on a green, don't play that shot. Pitch it out, so you can hit the green with the next shot and give your-self that putt for par. Doing this means you must *always play with the next shot in mind.*

Golf Strategy

A Preshot Routine for Putting

Don't make your pre-putt routine drawn out. Other than that, it doesn't matter what you do, *as long as your practice stroke is an identical motion to the real putt.* Too often players facing a 5-foot putt take a practice stroke that's just a stab.

A good practice stroke, then, should be a mirror of what you want to do when you hit the golf ball. During your practice stroke, concentrate on how far you need to take the putter back and through, in order to make the ball roll the proper distance.

FOCUS
Golf Strategy

The Key
to Putting

If you want to be a really good putter, practice the 40- to 50-foot putts. Try them with two or three different breaks across the green. Get a feel for putting uphill and go downhill at those distances. Find the hardest putts and practice all these. Then practice the 2- and 3- and 4-foot putts.

You can hit 15-foot putts all day on the practice green, and you won't get any better. Because out of 20 putts from 10 feet, the worst putter is only going to make one or two less than the best putter. The grain of the green, the bounces, the spike marks, the other stuff the ball hits — all of these can influence the roll of the ball and make the 10- or 15-foot putts much more of a matter of chance.

But if you can consistently lag it close to the hole from a long distance, and make 2- and 3- and 4-footers, you will be an excellent putter.

The Short Game Rescue

The 10- to 15-foot putt is the most overrated shot in golf — everybody thinks you've got to make it. But how many times in golf do you actually hit an iron shot 10 feet from the hole? Even the best players on their best days don't do it more than 10 times a round.

The key to a good round of golf is when you miss an iron shot and you're on the front edge of the green, say 50 feet from the hole, that you get it down in two. Or if you knock it stiff — within 4 feet— that you make that putt. Or if you miss a green, that you chip it within 4 feet and you make that for par. That's how you get rounds going, that's how low rounds are shot — not by making those 10- or 15-footers.

Nothing kills a round more than to hit it to 15 feet on each of the first three holes and not make one, then miss a green on the 4th hole, chip it to 4 feet, and miss the putt. It puts you one over par when you feel like you should be two under.

A lot of players will tell you that low rounds are generally shot when they start out struggling. Make a good up-and-down on one of the first two holes, a good two-putt from 30 feet, or a good save and all of a sudden instead of being one or two over, they're even. Then boom, 4th or 5th hole, they'll hit it close and make a birdie. Go one under, though, and they feel like they're off to the races.

Pitching Philosophy

You will be good with your pitch shots if you think: "minimum air time, maximum ground time."

In other words, you want to use the straightest-faced golf club possible for any given pitch shot. For example, if you're 10 feet off the green with 40 feet to the pin, take a 5-, 6-, or 7-iron. Then hit the ball so the natural loft of the club allows the ball to fly in the air just enough to land on the green to let the natural roll of the ball take it close to the hole.

Obviously, if you've got to pitch over a bunker, and you've only got 10 feet of green, you want to hit a high lob shot. But if you've got any room at all, pitch the ball to let it roll. That's the best chance you have of knocking it in or close. You don't see a lot of chip shots made where a guy hits a high lob with a lot of spin on the ball.

FOCUS
Golf Strategy

Short Game
Practice

If you want to knock shots off your game, spend as much time chipping and putting and pitching the ball as you do hitting balls on the practice range.

Helping Someone Believe

The Christian faith is based on faith to believe in miracles. Once a person is at that point, he can accept what has happened in Christ. The bedrock of the Christian faith rests on Christ paying the penalty for us — the fact that Jesus Christ was born, lived, and died and came back to life.

The next step is to get him to accept that it is a gift from God. You are saved by faith, not by what you do. Not by the amount of money you give, not by the good things you do, not by how many times you go to church.

> *"For by grace you have been saved through faith, and that not of yourselves; it is the gift of God, not of works, lest anyone should boast."*
> EPHESIANS 2:8,9

Those are two difficult issues to get by; you are never going to get anywhere explaining the Christian faith to someone unless God has prepared his or her heart. So I would say that praying for that person and establishing a relationship with that person has to happen first.

Life Strategy

Absolutes in Life

On the golf course, you will get some bad bounces. You might choose the right shot and hit it right, and still get a terrible result.

It's the same in life. You will trust someone, do the right thing, but people might hurt you and not live up to your expectations. *Bad things do happen to good people.*

> *"In our limited scope as humans we must accept the fact that earth is so temporal. God is so eternal."*

You have to go on, because of the prize we receive at the end when we're faithful. For those who believe, we will spend eternity with our Lord.

Faith and Winning

I'm a Christian. Does that mean I pray to God and He's supposed to let me make a shot, or He's supposed to make a putt for me? It doesn't happen that way. We have to look at Him and try to draw strength from what happens to us, because what happens, happens for a reason.

One of the things I like to share when I'm giving my testimony is that everything that's happened in my life — from the tournaments I've won to the tournaments I've blown, the bad shots, the good shots, everything in my life for the last 42 years — has happened for one reason: *for me to be right there to talk to those people on that day, telling them about my relationship with Jesus Christ*, and what He means to me.

Faith

Faith and Marriage

> *"I am the vine, and you are the branches.*
> *He who abides in me, and I in him, bears much fruit;*
> *for without me you can do nothing."*
>
> JOHN 15:5

I don't know how other people handle life on the Tour — if they are married — without a relationship with God. So many things can happen. As for my wife Kimberly and I, we need a relationship with Christ and faith in the Lord.

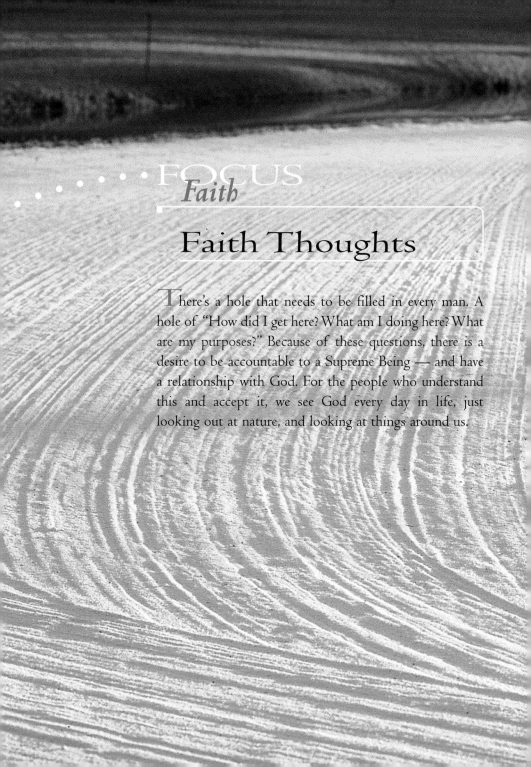

FOCUS
Faith

Faith Thoughts

There's a hole that needs to be filled in every man. A hole of "How did I get here? What am I doing here? What are my purposes?" Because of these questions, there is a desire to be accountable to a Supreme Being — and have a relationship with God. For the people who understand this and accept it, we see God every day in life, just looking out at nature, and looking at things around us.

The U.S. Open in 1994:
A Faith Lesson

I was at Oakmont. The 72nd hole of the U.S. Open, the last hole of the tournament. It was what every boy who plays golf dreams about, to have a putt on the last hole of the U.S. Open to win.

I had about a 4 1/2- or 5-foot putt straight up the hill with a little left-to-right break to win.

I was thinking the exact same thing I thought at Bay Hill. I said the exact same prayer to myself, and I hit the worst putt of my life. It didn't even come close.

What does that tell me? God's not going to do it for me, so I've got to get out there and perform. But He also knows what's best for me, and that's where the hindsight comes in.

If I had made that putt and won the U.S. Open it would have been great. But *God knows what is best for me,* and maybe I wasn't ready or mature enough at that point in my career to handle a win like that.

So I took something positive from that. *I could have looked at it as "I had a chance to win the Open and I blew it."*

Instead, I looked at it from the perspective that I had putted well for the previous 45 holes. I was out of the tournament on Friday, 6 over par, making the turn that day. I went 12 under the rest of the way. I shot a 64 on Saturday and came out of nowhere, making every putt to get into contention. The positive was that I gave myself a *chance* to win.

Faith on Tour

Like everybody else, I get carried away with my own importance at times. I get carried away with thinking that this is the most important thing I'm doing, what I'm doing at this very minute. In the long run, my faith takes a lot of pressure off of having to succeed out there. *I'm happy with who I am.* My career has given me more than I could have ever dreamed.

At times my faith makes it more difficult on Tour because I get convicted more when I mess up — if I don't do the right thing in a situation, like where I might have a chance to tell someone about my faith and I let it pass. Or if I'm in a competitive situation and I lose my temper and know people are watching.

Because the *best way to influence people for God is through your life.* You have to speak also and be willing to give an account of your faith when you're called. I'm not someone to go over and beat someone over the head with the Bible and say, "Repent today, or you're going to hell." I'm not confrontational that way. I feel like I have a better chance of someone believing me if they see happiness in my life, if they see me being good to my wife and being a responsible person.

Even though you are not saved by works, I think you should try to live your life in such a manner that you mirror God's love.

Finding Faith

I grew up in a Presbyterian church. I believed the stories in the Bible, and I believed in the Bible. But there was something missing . . . I just didn't have a personal relationship with Christ.

In 1983, my second full year on Tour, because of struggles with my game, I finally realized I needed to make a commitment.

It was in Milwaukee. I'd missed another cut — I think I'd made something like only $6,000 for the whole year —

> *"I will bless the Lord at all times;*
> *His praise shall continually be in my mouth."*
> PSALM 34:1

I was losing money. My wife and I had everything we owned in the trunk and backseat of a '78 Delta 88 Oldsmobile as we drove around the country. I just wasn't getting anywhere.

I remember coming back to the hotel room very despondent and coming to a decision: "I've got to change. *I can't get my self-worth from golf.* I know I need a personal relationship with Christ."

If you try to get your self-worth from what you do and what you achieve in life, it's never going to measure up. When things aren't going well, you're going to feel like you are worthless, and when things are going really well, the pleasure lasts a short time and then goes away.

First Tour Win

I started the Tour in 1983 and played full-time for 11 years before I finally won a tournament. When I finally won at Bay Hill in 1994, it was a great tournament to win because it was Arnold Palmer's tournament and everybody knows what he means to the game. It was probably one of the year's strongest fields on the PGA Tour, and Bay Hill is a long, tough golf course.

On the 16th fairway, I went for the green in two on a par five and I hit it over the back of the green. It was in long rough, but a relatively easy chip shot, and I didn't get it up and down for birdie.

At that point, I was tied for the lead, but Fuzzy Zoeller and Vijay Singh were behind me. They could both birdie that hole because they are both longer than me. So I figured I needed to make one more birdie on 17 or 18 to have a chance.

I got on the 17th, a long par three over water, and I hit it about 40 feet left of the pin. Safe shot. I figured this could be my best chance to make birdie. I knew ahead on 18, the pin was way right, over the lake. On that hole with a good tee shot, I would still have a 3- or 4-iron off a downhill lie to a narrow green, and have very little chance of getting it close — par is a good score on the last hole at Bay Hill.

So on 17, thinking birdie, I made a run at the putt and knocked it 6 or 7 feet past the hole. I remember standing over the next putt, saying, "Lord, just let me hit this putt to the best of my ability. I'm not going to pray that You make this putt for me, because that's not going to happen; I know I've got to hit it. Just give me the strength to make the best effort I can and accept the consequences."

I hit the putt, and it went in the hole. And then I make a good two-putt from about 40 feet on the 18th hole. So I finished par, par, and I'm in the clubhouse. They've both birdied 16 to go one shot up on me.

Fuzzy hits it in the water on 17 and makes double bogey. Vijay hits it to the same spot I did on the 17th green, but he three putts and then drives it in the rough on 18 and can't get it on the green from the rough. He makes bogey, and *I win the tournament.*

FOCUS *Player Profiles*

Larry Mize: 9.23.58

FAMILY: Wife, Bonnie; David (4.17.86);
Patrick (2.12.89); Robert (4.2.93)

RESIDENCE: Columbus, GA

COLLEGE: Georgia Tech • Turned professional in 1980

HOBBIES: Fishing, all sports, piano. Reduced his playtime
to spend more time with his family.

QUOTE: "I have to make sure that I am not so busy in golf that I
don't sit down and open His Word and read and pray with Him."

Scott Simpson: 9.17.55

FAMILY: Wife, Cheryl; Brea Yoshiko (10.10.82);
Sean Tokuzo (10.14.86)

RESIDENCE: San Diego, CA

COLLEGE: University of Southern California
Turned professional in 1977

HOBBIES: Bible study, family activities, exercise, reading. Spends
a great deal of time with his family during the season.

QUOTE: "It was just a matter of giving up my pride and saying, 'Christ, I do need You.' I
faced the fact I wasn't perfect; I needed Christ so I could be in Heaven for all time."

Loren Roberts: 6.24.55

FAMILY: Wife, Kimberly; Alexandria (10.14.86); Addison (10.15.91)

RESIDENCE: Germantown, TN

COLLEGE: Cal Poly San Luis Obispo
Turned professional in 1975

HOBBIES: Club-making, hunting, all sports

QUOTE: "Even though you are not saved by works, I think you
should try to live your life in such a manner that you mirror God's love."